My Cancer Days

Written by Courtney Filigenzi
Illustrated by Nicole Tadgell

Published by the American Cancer Society
250 Williams Street NW, Atlanta, GA 30303-1002
Copyright ©2016 American Cancer Society

Manufactured by RR Donnelley
Manufactured in Reynosa, Mexico
Job # 126618

5 4 3 2 1   16 17 18 19 20

Cover design and composition by La Shae V. Ortiz

Library of Congress Cataloging-in-Publication Data
Filigenzi, Courtney.
My cancer days / written by Courtney Filigenzi; illustrated by Nicole Tadgell.
     pages cm
Summary: "A young girl uses color to express her full range of emotions as she undergoes cancer treatment"
"Helps them understand that it's okay to let out their feelings"– Provided by publisher.
ISBN 978-1-60443-091-2 (hardback) – ISBN 1-60443-091-5 (hardcover)
[1. Cancer–Fiction. 2. Emotions–Fiction. 3. African Americans–Fiction.] I. Tadgell, Nicole, 1969- illustrator. II. Title.

PZ7.F4933My 2015
[Fic]–dc22   2015029871

American Cancer Society

Book Publishing Staff
Senior Director, Journals and Book Publishing:
    Esmeralda Galán Buchanan
Managing Editor: Rebecca Teaff, MA
Senior Editor: Jill Russell
Publishing Coordinator: Vanika Jordan, MSPub
Editorial Assistant: Amy Rovere

Cancer Control Programs and Services Staff
Senior Vice President: Chuck Westbrook
Managing Director, Content: Eleni Berger
Director, Cancer Information: Louise Chang, MD

Quantity discounts on bulk purchases of this book are available. Contact us at **trade.sales@cancer.org**
for more information.

Dedicated with love to the bravest and youngest cancer warriors and their families. May your hope never falter, your fear never prevail, and your dreams all come true.   –*Courtney*

My life has been forever touched by the generosity of patients, families, doctors, and volunteers involved in children's cancer treatment and support. Thank you for letting me in and sharing your lives.

Very special thanks to Dr. Naheed Usmani, the University of Massachusetts Medical School Sidekicks Program, and to all the kids and families at Why Me and Sherry's House.   –*Nicole*

Earlier this year, I found out that I am sick.

I have something called cancer,

and it can be **really**, **really** bad.

Some days, **I feel scared.**

These are my purple times.

I wonder if I will be okay and what
will happen to my family
and me if I'm not.

I worry about all the doctor visits
and treatments I need. Sometimes they scare me.

It's okay to feel purple.

Some days, **I feel blue...**

I feel sad and alone.

Sometimes other people's germs can make me really sick,
so I can't see my friends and family. I miss them.

I just want everything to be normal again.

It's okay to feel blue.

Some days, **I feel green**...

I feel jealous of healthy kids and their families.

I wonder why I have to be the one who is sick.

Why can't my life be more like other people's?

It's okay
to feel green.

Some days, **I feel just fine.**

These are my yellow days...
happy days that seem normal and good.

I feel a little bit better.
I can play with my friends and do the things I love to do.

I love my

yellow days.

But then, my **orange** days come…

I start to feel bad again, and I don't want to believe that I am still sick.

I want to pretend it's not really happening.

It's okay to feel orange.

Some days, **I feel red** inside…

I get angry. I want to yell. I feel so mad that sometimes
I say and do things I shouldn't.

Then, I realize how much I love my life and my family.
I have so many feelings I don't know what to do.

It's okay
to feel red.

But I don't have to feel guilty or ashamed about my feelings.
They are a part of me. And it's okay to let my feelings out.

I can hope that someday…

I will be well again.

About the Author

Courtney Filigenzi is the award-winning author of
Let My Colors Out. She graduated from Towson University
with a major in biology and a minor in chemistry. Courtney
lives in Woodstock, Maryland, with her husband and two sons.

About the Illustrator

Nicole Tadgell is the award-winning illustrator of more than
twenty picture books, including *In the Garden with Dr. Carver*.
Having lost a sister to childhood illness, she was very moved
by the theme of this book. In the course of her research, Nicole
visited pediatric cancer patients and their families, both in
hospital and home settings. Seeing their natural joy, hope, and resilience was
inspiring. Visit her online at www.nicoletadgell.blogspot.com.

Other Children's Books Published by the American Cancer Society
Available everywhere books are sold and online at **cancer.org/bookstore**

And Still They Bloom: A Family's Journey of Loss and Healing

Because… Someone I Love Has Cancer

Imagine What's Possible: Use the Power of Your Mind to Take Control of Your Life During Cancer

Kids' First Cookbook: Delicious-Nutritious Treats to Make Yourself!

Let My Colors Out

The Long and the Short of It: A Tale About Hair

Mom and the Polka-Dot Boo-Boo

Nana, What's Cancer?

No Thanks, but I'd Love to Dance: Choosing to Live Smoke Free

Our Dad Is Getting Better

Our Mom Has Cancer (available in hard cover and paperback)

Our Mom Is Getting Better

What's Up with Bridget's Mom? Medikidz Explain Breast Cancer (available in English and Spanish)

What's Up with Jo? Medikidz Explain Brain Tumors
(available in English and Spanish)

What's Up with Lyndon? Medikidz Explain Osteosarcoma
(available in English and Spanish)

What's Up with Richard? Medikidz Explain Leukemia
(available in English and Spanish)

What's Up with Tiffany's Dad? Medikidz Explain Melanoma
(available in English and Spanish)

What's Up with Jerome's Grandad? Medikidz Explain Prostate Cancer
(available in English and Spanish)

What's Up with Our Dad? Medikidz Explain Colorectal Cancer
(available in English and Spanish)

What's Up with Sam's Grandma? Medikidz Explain Lung Cancer
(available in English and Spanish)

Visit **cancer.org/bookstore** for a full listing of books
published by the American Cancer Society.